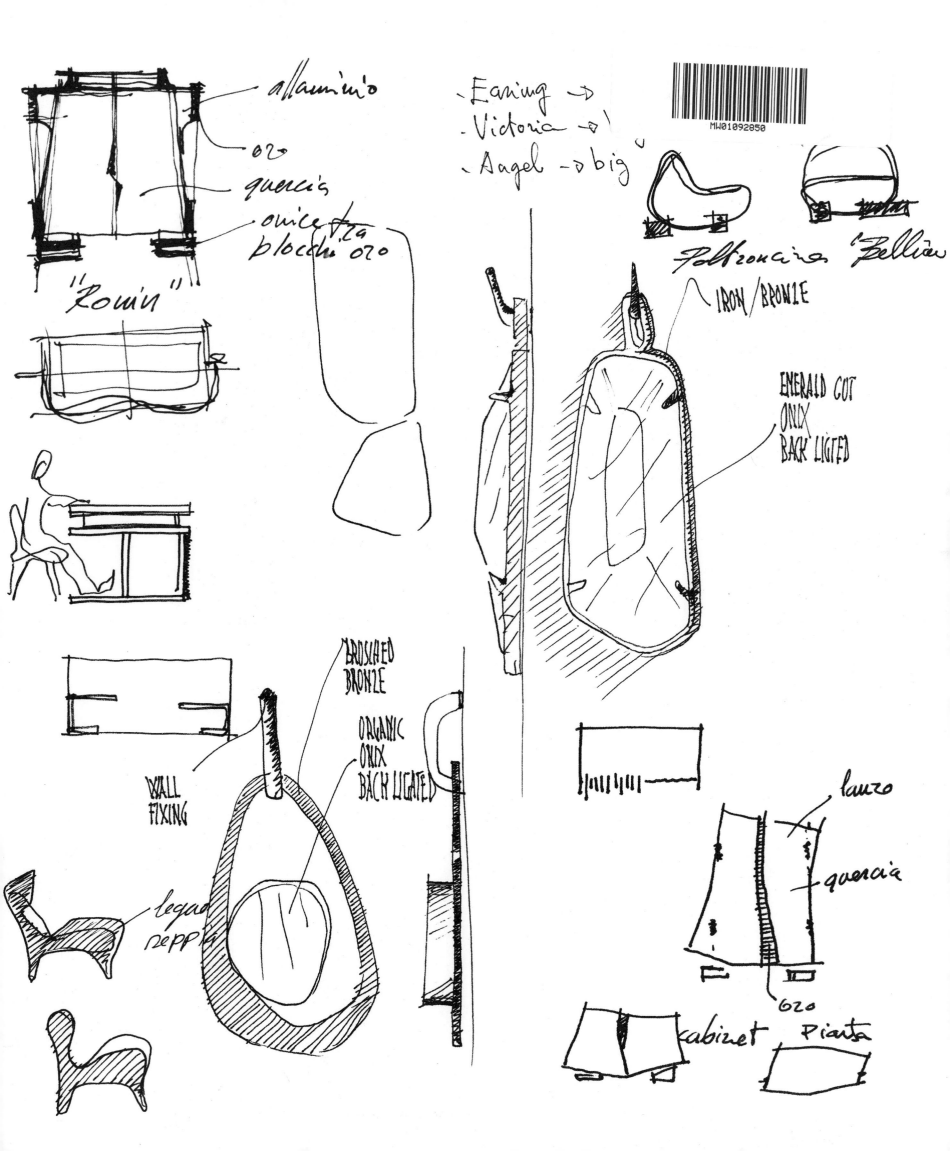

alluminio

oro

quercia

onice + la
blocchi oro

"Romin"

Earring →
Victoria →
Angel → big

Poltroncina "Bellini"

IRON/BRONZE

EMERALD CUT
ONIX
BACK LIGTED

BROSHED
BRONZE

ORGANIC
ONIX
BACK LIGTED

WALL
FIXING

legno
nepp'

lanzo

quercia

oro

kabinet   Pianta

ACHILLE SALVAGNI

ACHILLE SALVAGNI

PILAR VILADAS

Rizzoli
NEW YORK

New York · Paris · London · Milan

Achille Salvagni may be known throughout the world as a daring, highly original, and successful furniture designer, but he is so much more. First and foremost, he is an architect, a Roman whose understanding of the art of fine living is translated through the exquisite environments he creates. What distinguishes him from his peers is his insistence on design-

ing nearly everything for a project and his uncompromising refusal to employ anything but the finest materials—bronze, exotic woods, precious stones, and sumptuous textiles. Over the years he has collaborated with masters of woodworking, stonecutting, and bronze who make unique pieces in small workshops all over Italy (including the craftsmen who have served the Vatican for generations). What is unusual is that he likes to challenge these skilled artisans, asking them to employ their age-old techniques in unorthodox ways to create distinctive contemporary pieces. Though most designers will slice thin sheets of alabaster and cobble them together when creating translucent sconces, not Salvagni. Following architect Pierre Chareau, he insists on slabs carved from a solid block that are then held together by a solid bronze frame. The effect is nothing short of spectacular.

Since 2013 Maison Gerard has been proud to showcase Salvagni's creations: ravishingly beautiful cabinets, consoles, tables, chairs, mirrors, lighting, and accessories. They resemble the work of no other creator. He is truly a design couturier. As a gallery whose origins are in fine French Art Deco, it is no surprise that we have embraced Salvagni's works, which share the same attention to detail and neverending search for refinement. Much like a Jacques-Émile Ruhlmann or a Jules Leleu, Salvagni can be considered a contemporary *décorateurs ensembliers*—masterfully creating entire rooms with nothing but original works. In the 1920s and 1930s, designers would collaborate in the design of the interiors of grand ocean liners. Not unlike these masters, Salvagni has found in the design of the interiors of superyachts his floating playground.

BENOIST F. DRUT Today he is a household name in both Europe and America, and his projects have been published worldwide. He has won several international prizes for his work. Yet he is happiest in Rome with his wife and children. He is a curious, kind person, a gentleman in every respect who also happens to be a genius. It is my honor to be his friend and to share his creativity with you.

In the seventeen years since Achille Salvagni founded his practice, Achille Salvagni Architetti, in

Rome, the architect and designer has become known for his sophisticated interiors, including

apartments in New York and Palm Beach, a flat overlooking Holland Park in London, and an

apartment in Paris. He has become one of the

INTRODUCTION

world's preeminent designers of yacht interiors,

for which he has won numerous awards. And his limited-edition furniture, lighting, and object designs

are sought after both by collectors and by his fellow designers for their own projects.

Stylistically, Salvagni is an avowed modernist; his work displays an elegant economy of means

that is utterly contemporary. Yet his work consistently bears the weight of history—not in overt

references, but in its material richness, impeccable craftsmanship, and deeply layered narrative.

For instance, the elliptical shape of his Roma cabinet refers to a form commonly found in Roman

architecture and urban design, but here it is almost minimalist, in contrast to its sumptuous mate-

rials: French-polished walnut; bronze for the top and for the legs, which are shaped like a pope's

miter; and gilded bronze for the edges of the top, the handles, and the arrow-shaped hinges,

which evoke the Roman Empire's military history.

His inspirations range from the work of the audacious Baroque architect Francesco Borromini—a

skylight in one of Salvagni's yacht interiors echoes the dynamic oval shape of the dome of

Borromini's church of San Carlo alle Quattro Fontane in Rome—to the modern but sumptuous

furniture designs of twentieth-century Italian masters like Gio Ponti, Tomaso Buzzi, and Paolo Buf-

fa. (All three embodied—like Salvagni—the Italian tradition of architects designing everything from

buildings to light fixtures.) The last three "embody the essence of being Italian, paying attention to

Italian history, but not being overwhelmed by it, and being extremely refined and sophisticated,"

he says—and his designs are, similarly, inspired by history, yet very much of our time. "If you want

to look at the future," Salvagni says, "you need to know the past."

Salvagni can trace his own interest in design and architecture back to his childhood. Born in

Rome, he grew up in Latina, a city about forty-five miles southeast of Rome, which was founded

(as Littoria) in 1932 by the Fascists, on a marsh that many before them, from the ancient Romans

onward, had tried and failed to drain. The Italian Rationalist style dominated the city's architecture.

Salvagni's father, whom he calls "my first point of reference," was in construction and developed a specialty in building wineries. From the time Salvagni was four or five, he would travel with his father, who, he says, "treated me like an adult. He was happy to share his work with me; he would take me to building sites. My mother said I kept a hammer and screwdriver under my pillow at night, and my father gave me a small tool belt that was made by a saddler." When Salvagni was eight, he got a Christmas gift of a worktable with a vise; it had its own room in the family's house.

Salvagni's school notebooks reveal that, as early as age ten, he was drawing designs for furniture. At that age, he says, "I knew I'd be an architect. I never considered anything else." At first, the choice didn't please his father. As Salvagni recalls, "He said that I had to study something I could make a living from, but I insisted." Eventually, Salvagni proved himself, and his father, who now lives outside Rome with Salvagni's mother, "sees the future with my eyes. We speak every day."

Salvagni attended the Sapienza University of Rome, where he got his architecture degree in 1998, and absorbed the lessons of the dazzling historic feast that is the Roman built environment. Eventually, however, being surrounded by so much history began to feel stifling, and Salvagni applied for grants to study abroad. He won two—one to Oxford, and one to the Royal Institute of Technology in Stockholm. He chose the latter because "I wanted to breathe," he says. The time he spent there, fourteen months, "was the happiest period of my life—I felt free." The school was open twenty-four hours a day, so that students could sketch or make models at all hours. Salvagni was fascinated by the Scandinavian modernism of architects like Alvar Aalto, Erik Gunnar Asplund, and Sigurd Lewerentz. Their work, he says, "has the vision, and an impressive sensitivity to detail and the human being, and that's something that will never leave me." During his stay, Salvagni went to Finland and saw every one of Aalto's buildings. When he visited Aalto's own house and saw one of the architect's suits hanging in a closet, Salvagni touched the jacket and was moved to tears. For him, the most influential elements of Aalto's work are "genius loci—the roots of a design, in which everything refers to Finland; the curve; and rationalism with a human quality," he explains.

After college, Salvagni worked part-time for an architecture office and part-time with a friend and fellow architect, Riccardo Sanchini. But he chafed at what he considered the inefficiency of a big office and—having made more money in six months on his freelance projects than he had as an employee—decided to go out on his own, despite his employers' offer to quadruple his salary if he would stay. Sanchini joined him.

Within a year, Salvagni's office had grown from two people to eight. Needing more space, he found an abandoned warehouse for horse-drawn carriages on the Palatine Hill—with eighteen-foot ceilings and sand on the floor—and Salvagni put all the money he had into renovating it. There was more space than he needed at the time, but, he says, "I always look ahead, and I figured the firm would grow, and that I'd rather suffer now than have to look for a larger space later." The firm, which now numbers twenty-four people, is still there; six years ago, Salvagni bought the space next door, doubling the office's amount of square footage.

The variety of Salvagni's early projects was typical for a young architect trying to establish a practice: "If I were too picky," he says, "I wouldn't survive." His work for his previous employer had included a chain of supermarkets, and once he went out on his own, the client came to him and asked him to continue his work for them. In three years, he recalls, he designed around one hundred supermarkets, followed by an apartment in Rome and a headquarters for the supermarket company. One of the two brothers who owned the company bought a yacht and asked Salvagni to design the interiors for free; the client argued that he was taking a risk on a novice. "He thought I was overqualified to design supermarkets," Salvagni says, "but had to start somewhere." Crediting the pragmatism that he inherited from his father, Salvagni agreed to the deal; the yacht won first prize for the best interior at the Cannes Boat Show in 2006, and soon Salvagni's staff numbered fifteen. "I had started designing supermarkets because it was a job," he says, "but if I hadn't worked on the supermarkets, I might never have designed a yacht." He has since designed more than twenty yacht interiors.

It is a category that poses its own challenges. A yacht's interior spaces are seldom orthogonal, Salvagni argues, because the structure of a yacht is more complex than that; he maintains that you can't just design and furnish a yacht's interior as you would a house. Salvagni admires the all-wood interiors of the America's Cup yachts from the 1920s and has emulated their approach in some of his own designs. "I try to avoid corners, and shiny surfaces, which adversely affect people's balance. You have to increase the level of comfort on a yacht," Salvagni says. "Conventional furniture only goes so far; a yacht needs custom pieces." This includes designing furniture with a lower center of gravity, and—since the ceilings are lower on yachts—avoiding barstools, which can make people feel queasy. When Salvagni uses vintage pieces, they may be chairs by Gio Ponti or Jules Leleu, that were designed for ocean liners, with seats that are lower to the floor. Closet doors have hidden magnets to hold them shut in rough weather, and drawers are secured with manual latches so they don't fly open. Salvagni began designing furniture specifically for yachts in 2010, for the 225-foot *Numptia*. His work was so successful—the yacht won an award for the best interior and furniture—that people started asking him to adapt these pieces for use in other spaces.

When Salvagni was commissioned to design the interiors of an apartment on Fifth Avenue in New York, he started to look for a gallery in the city that specialized in limited-edition design. Through his publicist at the time, Harriet Weintraub, he was introduced to Benoist Drut, one of the founders of the renowned gallery Maison Gerard, who was immediately impressed by Salvagni's designs—both for furniture and for the Aldus collection of objects, a collaboration between Salvagni and Fabio Gnessi. The gallery showed them at the Collective Design fair in 2013, and he is now one of its most important designers. And in the fall of 2015, Salvagni opened his own gallery, Achille Salvagni Atelier, on Grafton Street in London's exclusive Mayfair district. The gallery showcases his work in a series of thematic exhibitions, like *Apollo*, *Kyoto*, and *Sahara*. Salvagni considers the sumptuous materials and obsessive craftsmanship of his furniture—for instance, a handle on a cabinet door that is made of gilded bronze and semiprecious stone—as jewelry. "I'm obsessed by details, jewel-like details, like parchment over wood, or marble and bronze handles," he explains. So when it came time to choose a neighborhood for his London gallery, he said, "I wanted to be among fine jewelers."

But beautifully designed interiors and furnishings are only part of Salvagni's approach. "I feel that my DNA is an architect's," he says. "I can't help evaluating volumes and the flow of space. I start with plans and elevations, and go from there. I'm not a decorator—it's a part of my work, but not the essence. I shape and sculpt the space; the architecture needs to be a piece of art."

Once he conceptualizes the space, Salvagni starts to shape its narrative. "I start with a dream about the idea of the interior," he says. "I gather as much imagery as I can, since one of the most important things a designer can do is to have documentation and points of reference. You need to know the rules before you can break them. So now, for instance, I can play with a curved line because I studied so much of Aalto's work." After that, he says, "The theme comes next. I collect a large number of inspiration images and fix them in my brain. I learn a vocabulary, and spend a couple of days being bombarded by these messages—and then I tell my own story."

Salvagni also sees himself—as do many designers—as something of a psychologist. "The client's expectations are very important," he says. "I fulfill them in my own style, but it's the client's point of view that is most important to me." Still, when he needs to, he is able to manage those expectations. The owner of a yacht told Salvagni that he wanted an Art Deco design. "Step by step, I moved him to a different place, to what he had in mind but could not express. Clients don't always have the tools to explain what they really want," he adds. "I spend a lot of quality time with my clients before starting a project; we talk about what they like and need."

But prospective clients who are looking for *le style Salvagni* will be disappointed. "Many times I've been contacted by people who've seen my work published, and want the same thing," he says. "I say, 'No way—your project will be one of a kind. I can't move ahead without references, which is why I can't create an interior in a specific style. I need the history of what I'm dealing with, to know what others did before me, and then I find my own way."

That way, however, starts with an inclusive vision. "Beauty leads, and beauty guides," Salvagni says. "That's why I could put an iPhone on a seventeenth-century console, and there won't be a conflict. The easiest way is to collect beautiful things, and this has nothing to do with their value," he explains. "It's more about harmony and the soul of the space. I can mix my own designs with other contemporary pieces, or with vintage or antique pieces, and art—they're all important. Sometimes I conceive an entire project around the art. I'm not a one-man show."

A notable example of Salvagni's passion for art is his own apartment in Rome, which he shares with his wife, Valentina, a law professor, and his children, Gaetano and Vittoria. The apartment, which overlooks the teahouse of the eighteenth-century Villa Albani, is filled with works by noted modern and contemporary Italian artists—including Giuseppe Uncini, Gianni Piacentino, and Jannis Kounellis—and pieces by Ilya and Emilia Kabakov and Zhang Huan, among others. Salvagni orchestrates an artful mix between these works and furniture by designers like Paolo Buffa and Tomaso Buzzi, as well as other vintage and antique pieces and Salvagni's own designs—among them, a black side table with arrow-shaped legs and an upholstered chair named after his daughter, both of which are in the living room. For the dining room, he designed a table with parchment-covered legs and a black glass top edged in bronze.

In the master bedroom, a print of Richard Avedon's iconic photograph *Dovima with Elephants* hangs next to a pair of photos, taken by a researcher in the 1940s, of the last two cannibals on Fiji; Salvagni found them in a flea market there. The contrast between the glamorous model and the cannibals is startling and illustrates Salvagni's knack for putting unlikely elements together, as with the nineteenth-century plaster bust, in the apartment's winter garden, which Salvagni adorned with a pair of goggles.

By the time this book is published, Salvagni will have completed his first design from the ground up, for a sleek, spacious contemporary house in Miami—with materials that include white plaster, travertine, and verde alpi marble—as well as a townhouse renovation on New York's Upper East Side. Across town, he is at work on another townhouse, this one on Riverside Drive, to which he will add space underground and on the roof. His current project roster is evenly divided among residential interiors, yachts, and the design of furniture and objects.

Salvagni believes that the role of the designer today is shaped by the idea that "design transforms, creates, and shapes something that needs to be lived with, in the most beautiful way. We've always had design, since the Neanderthal man. Creating a cup, a hammer, or a sword is to design, but today we're overwhelmed by different messages. Design is an aesthetic approach to a functional need, and the role of the designer is to enrich the experience." And the key to this kind of enrichment, Salvagni says, is beauty. "Its value is to affect human beings, and let them absorb something that will never leave. Beauty is not connected to time."

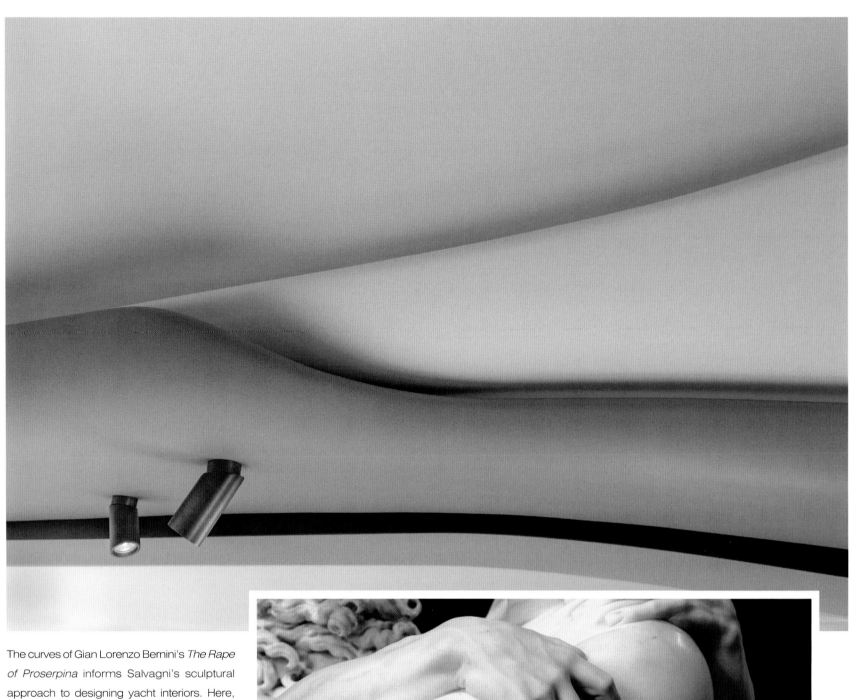

The curves of Gian Lorenzo Bernini's *The Rape of Proserpina* informs Salvagni's sculptural approach to designing yacht interiors. Here, wood with bronze inlay, lacquered fiberglass, and leather over fiberglass cover up mechanical equipment and beams in the ceiling of an Azimut Grande twenty-seven-meter yacht.

One of the most impressive aspects of Salvagni's work is that it is simultaneously modern in philosophy and traditional in execution. The formal rigor and restraint of his interiors and furniture go hand in hand not just with sumptuous materials and impeccable craftsmanship, but also with a fluidity of line that produces—no matter how pared-down the room or the object—a sensual softness that is irresistible.

HARMONY

Of course, "luxurious" sensuality is a hallmark of the Italian Baroque: just think of the architecture of Francesco Borromini or Gian Lorenzo Bernini, or the latter's voluptuous marble sculptures. It also distinguishes the work of Italian architects and designers of the 1940s though the 1960s—like Gio Ponti, Paolo Buffa, or Luigi Caccia Dominioni—whose pieces Salvagni frequently uses in his own projects. But these designers, Salvagni believes, were influenced, as he was—in his travels to Sweden and Finland after his university studies—by Scandinavian modernism, particularly the work of Alvar Aalto, who was himself influenced by Erik Gunnar Asplund and Sigurd Lewerentz, and the way they "inserted soft shapes, and bent and softened the lines" of modernist architecture. This approach, Salvagni argues, "makes space more human, and creates a sense of comfort. Our bodies don't have corners."

Curves are often a starting point in Salvagni's designs: "I shape the space, then decorate it," he explains. He often rounds the corners of a room or where a wall meets the ceiling; in one yacht interior, he created a sculptural soffit (to conceal mechanical systems) that was inspired by the sensual rendering of human flesh in Bernini's sculpture *The Rape of Proserpina*. Salvagni designs walls of wood panels that seem to fold softly at their edges, as if the material were pliable rather than rigid. He also creates softness through layering, as he did on the yacht *Numptia*, where one warm, wood-paneled room looks into another, inspired by the interiors of a villa that were designed by the great Renzo Mongiardino. Salvagni's enfilade of framed views creates a dreamlike effect.

FLUIDITY & SOFTNESS

Sensual curves define Salvagni's designs for the Tato, Vittoria, and Gae chairs; the overlapping forms of his Clouds mirror; and the undulating doors of his Silk and Antinoo cabinets. And Salvagni takes the idea of curves to its most playful in his Bubbles lights, where artful clusters of spheres of gilt bronze and onyx look as if they might defy their own weight, and just float away.

Salvagni's inspiration for the shape of the fireplace in an NYC pied-á-terre is from the architecture of the Rosario Candela–designed building located at 19 East 76th Street in Manhattan.

Sometimes it seems as if interior design today veers between extremes when it comes to color, producing rooms that are either relentlessly monochromatic or riotously—almost chaotically—colorful. Salvagni's approach to color, on the other hand, is one of strategic layering. Against a consistently neutral backdrop, he adds colors that range from subtle to vibrant, but which never reveal themselves at first glance; the closer you look, the more color you see.

COLOR

"Color gives identity to a space," Salvagni says. "I stay away from monochromatic schemes, as they're nearly absent in nature; even in the forest, a red flower will be a focal point. The trend toward gray or beige interiors disturbs me," he adds. His approach is influenced by the delicate colors of Giotto's paintings, or the more intense, rich tones used by the Renaissance painter Agnolo Bronzino. Salvagni believes that to appreciate the essence of something—a chair, a vase, a painting—you need to be able to "read the edges." He prefers to create a neutral palette for the room itself, so the colors—of furnishings, fabrics, or objects—stand out, creating focal points that reinforce the room's identity and transmit a sense of liveliness and joy. And for Salvagni, some of the most compelling focal points are works of art. "I rarely use pattern," he says, "I prefer that art plays that role." For example, in an apartment on Fifth Avenue, the pale neutral palette of the room provides a foil for the bright red painting by Lucio Fontana that hangs above the fireplace; the light backdrop makes the art appear even more vivid.

The art can also guide the choice of colors for fabrics, Salvagni explains. For instance, in the Fifth Avenue living room, the red of the Fontana is echoed (although not literally) in the orange of the accent pillows on the sofas and in the deep red of the leather covering the chairs, by Jacques Adnet, that flank the card table at the window. In Salvagni's own living room, small areas of deep yellow in the painting by Emilia and Ilya Kabakov are reflected in the gold velvet that covers the two chairs—designed in the 1950s by Nino Zoncada for the ocean liner *Raffaello*—on either side of it.

EXPRESSION THEORY

Salvagni credits the legendary designer Renzo Mongiardino as his inspiration for this strategy: "He always found a fabric connected to the art in the room." These connections, however, are less direct than they are subliminal; Salvagni's skilled, sophisticated integration of art and color in his interiors creates a visual and emotional synergy that makes the experience of these spaces that much richer.

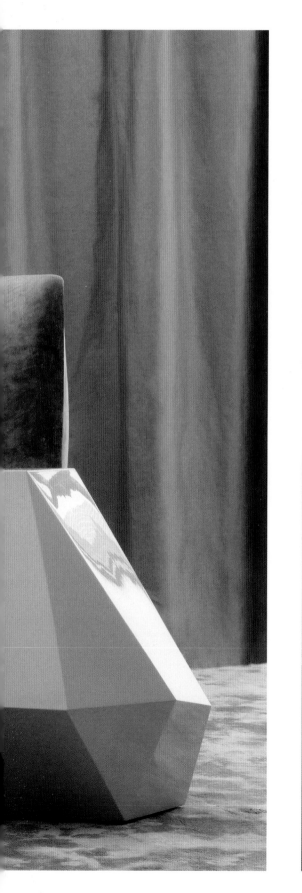

A fresco from the House of Augustus in Rome depicting the ancient city of Pompeii inspired this London interior, where Salvagni brought together materials including marble, bronze, and walnut to create stunning pieces with historical references.

A fresco by Raffaellino del Colle representing Saint Leo the Great from Oratorio di San Leo in Sansepolcro inspired the base of Salvagni's Roma cabinet. Each cast bronze leg is shaped like the Pope's tiara.

Design and craftsmanship are inseparable; you can't have one without the other. Salvagni has been exposed to both since childhood, and this exposure had a formative effect on his work. And for Salvagni, Rome, where he attended university, is "the mother of every reference to craftsmanship," he says, referring to the city's seemingly endless examples of peerless work in stone, bronze,

CRAFTSMANSHIP

and wood. His design for an apartment in the city's historic Palazzo Colonna, close to a decade ago, "opened doors" to high-end craftspeople with whom he has worked ever since. He explains that such craftspeople are almost like a secret club and that, for instance, "a lampshade maker will tell you who the best bronze person is." Indeed, Salvagni works with a man "who does the bronzes for the Vatican City," and he accompanies his preferred stone carver to the quarries of Carrara to choose blocks of marble. "I want to go to the origin of the material, and I like to get my hands dirty," he adds. But in one case, the craftspeople are not quite as accessible. The exquisite embroidery in Salvagni's projects is done by cloistered nuns in a convent near Rome. "You can't see them face-to-face," he says, "but you can talk to them through a screen, as if you were in a confessional." Salvagni's expressions of these materials take many different forms. He uses bronze for the curved feet of his Roma cabinet, as well as for the cabinet's slender, arrow-shaped hinges. But bronze takes on a completely different personality in the base of the Tango console, where it becomes a kinetic composition of angled legs, inspired by the movements of tango dancers. It can be jewel-like, as in the handles, which are combined with semiprecious stone, of his Palatino and Nerone cabinets, or somewhat disquieting, as in the sharply pointed finial of the Lancea lamp, which contrasts with its sumptuous shade of fabric meticulously stitched around its curved ribs. Wood is bent, employing the same technology used to make violins, into sinuous, silky contours for cabinet doors, or it becomes the faceted geometric forms of Salvagni's Emerald tables.

ARTISTIC GESTURE

Onyx becomes the glowing, translucent shades for sconces and chandeliers—like the Darts chandelier, where bronze "darts" seem to pierce the stone shade, which is carved to look almost like draped fabric. In Salvagni's imagination, materials become their most luxurious, and sometimes their most unlikely, selves. And this is what makes his designs so unfailingly seductive.

The "Ditchley portrait" of Queen Elizabeth I by Marcus Gheeraerts the Younger informed the shape of the handmade and stitched Japanese silk lampshade that adorns the Lancea lamps and was created by an eighty-five-year-old woman who was formerly the assistant of Renzo Mongiardino.

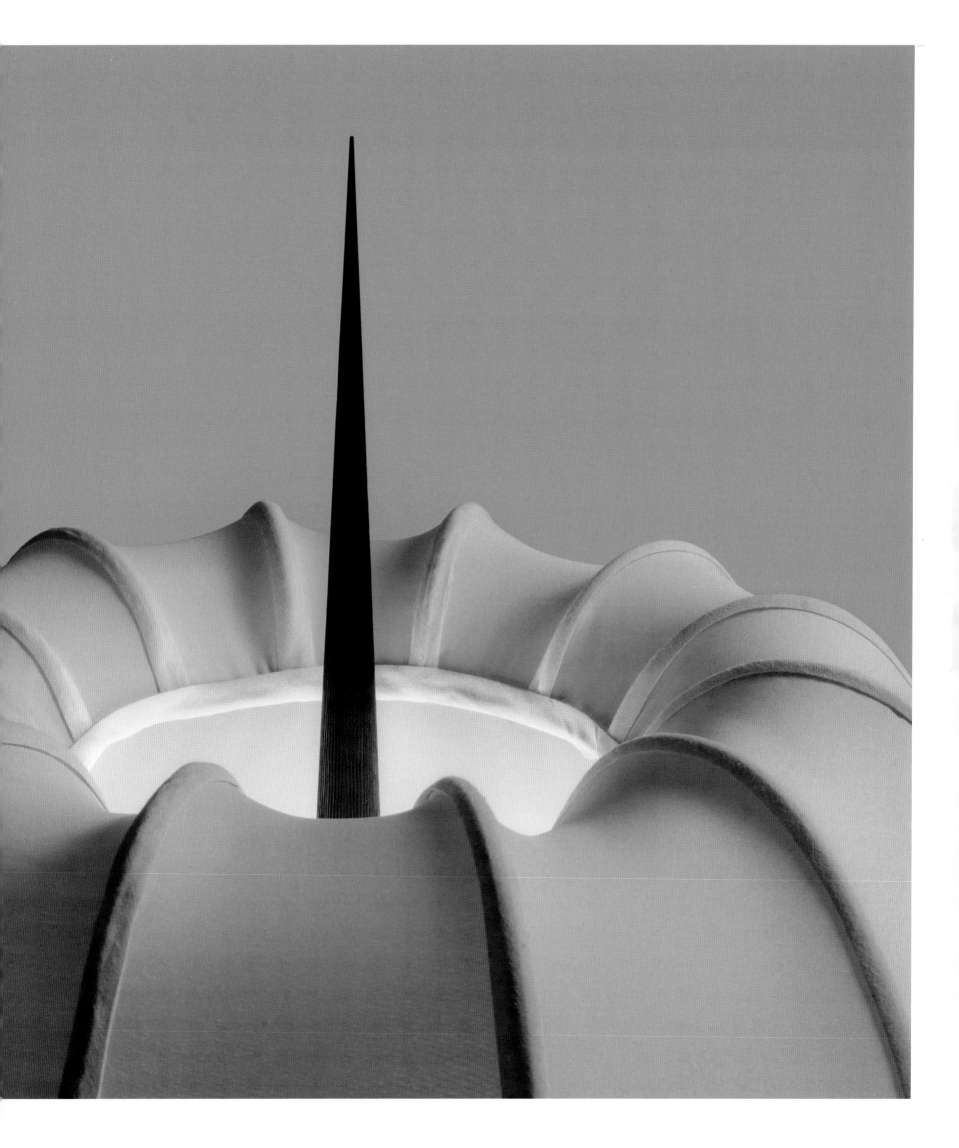

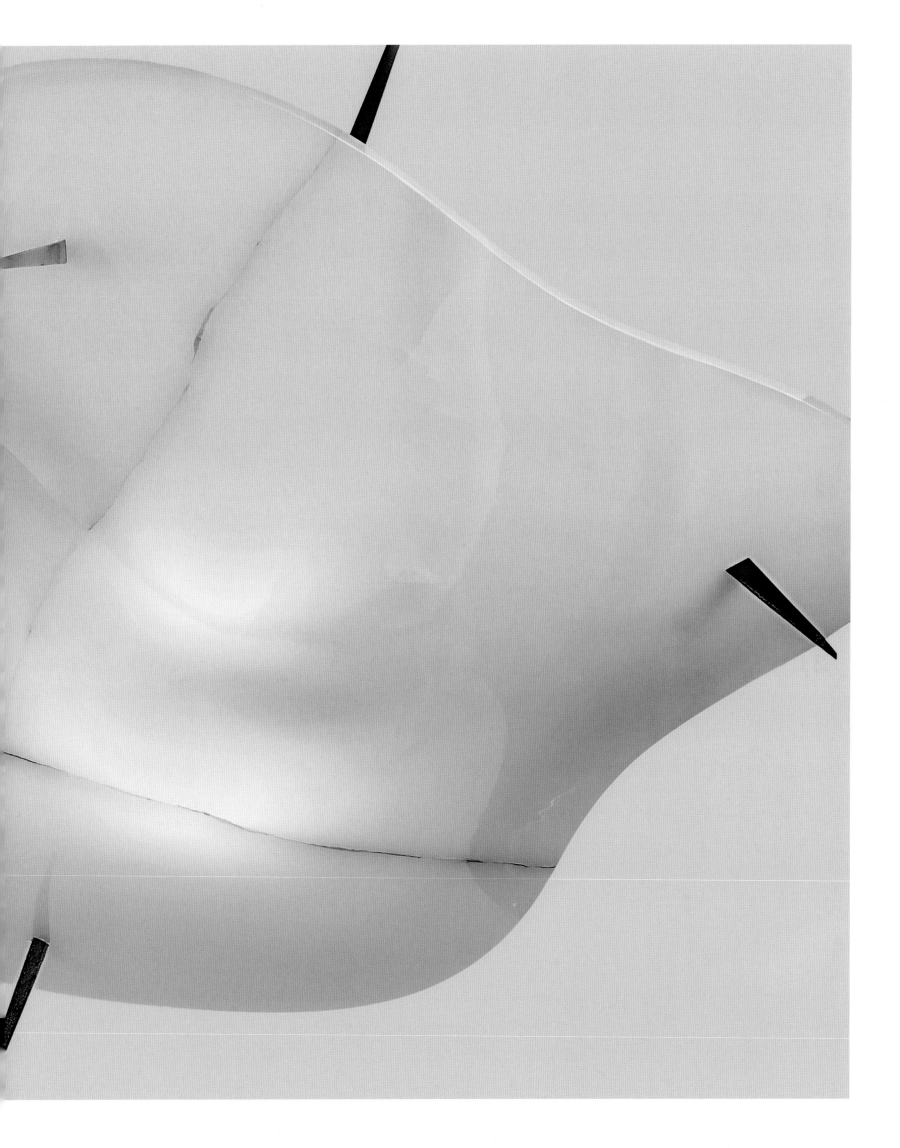

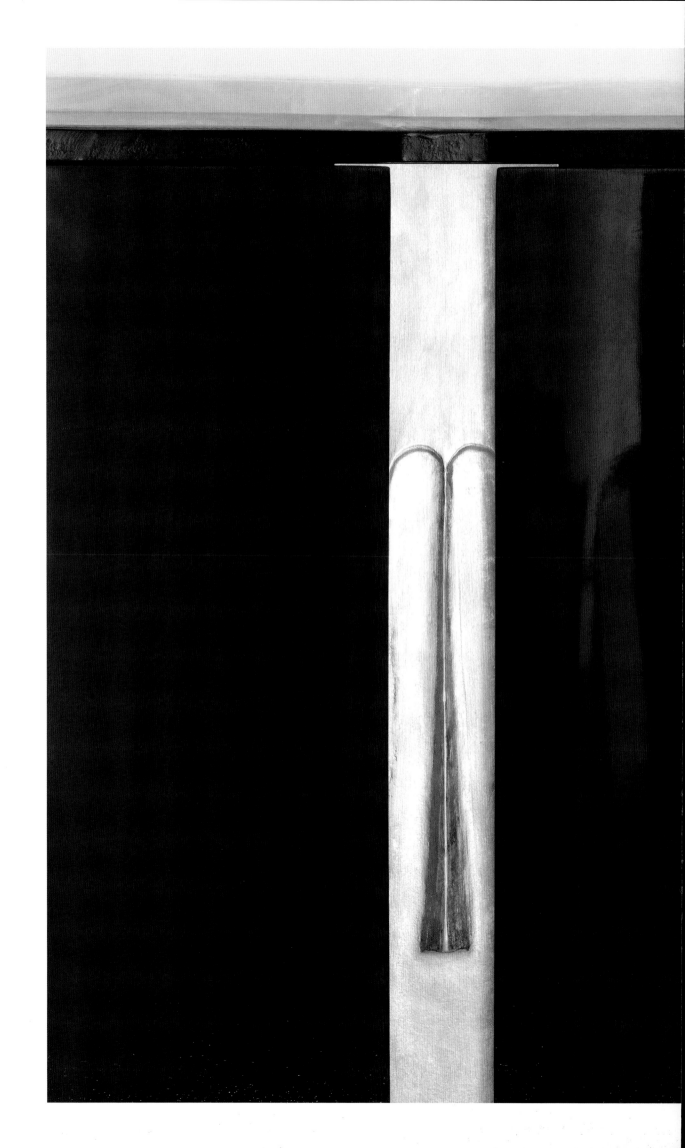

Antinous, the beautiful Greek youth believed to be the secret lover of the Roman Emperor Hadrian, inspired the cabinet for which it's named. This relationship is represented in a subtle face on the bronze panel in the center of the credenza's two doors.

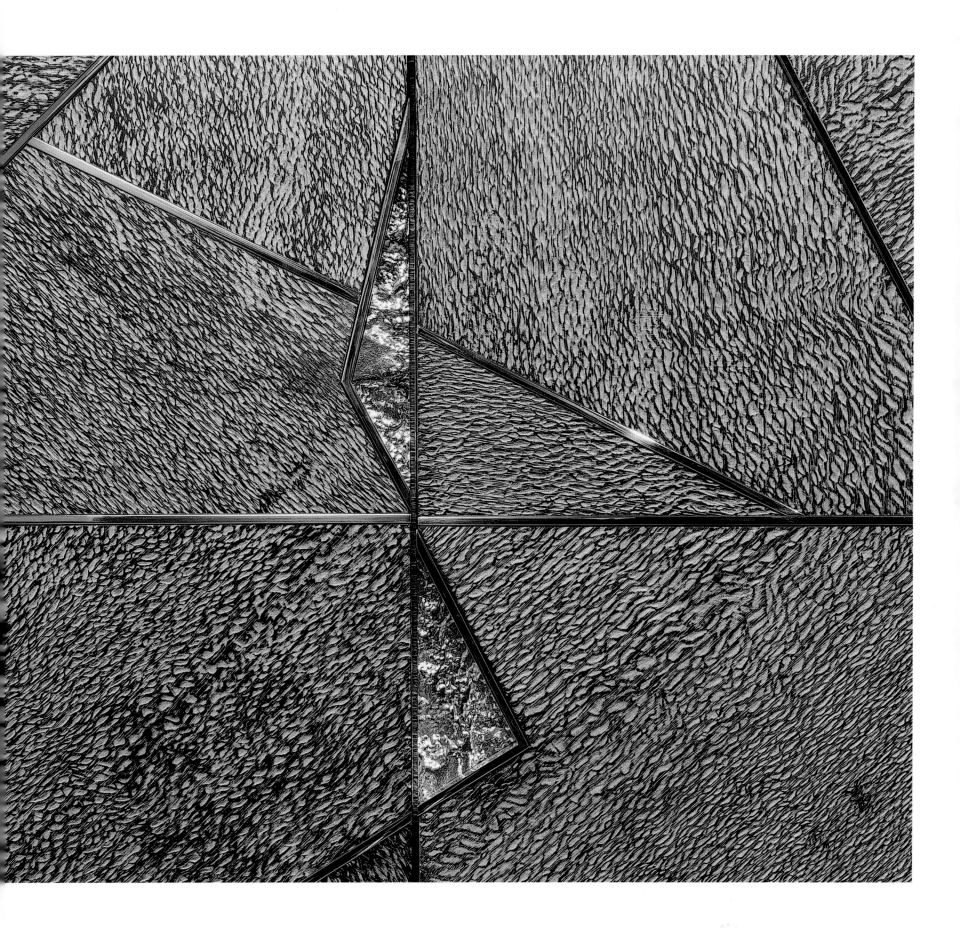

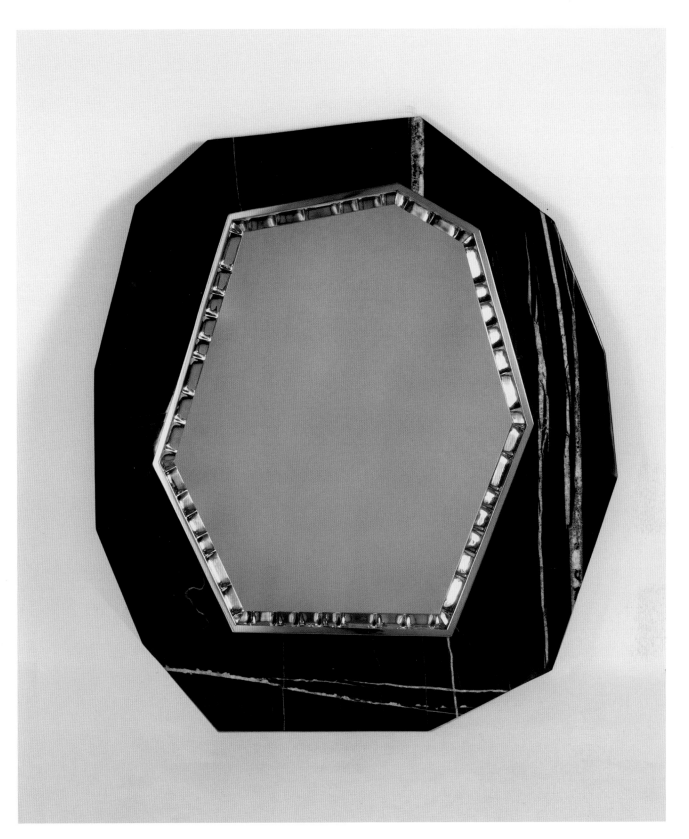

The influence of the mosaics in the adulatory vault Santa Costanza Church in Rome can be seen in the staircase of this Rossinavi superyacht, including the curved wooden panels with a metallic-looking finish.

The saying "You have to know the rules in order to break them" is a favorite of Salvagni's. As elegant as his work is, simply playing it safe holds no appeal; Salvagni is the first to admit that "there's something that drives me to do things that are a little crazy, that make a space more vibrant." He likes to look at a space from a different point of view, to subvert expec- **AUDACITY** tations, and to move clients beyond their own expectations. Some of Salvagni's most audacious decisions have been made for the yacht interiors he designs. For the *Endeavour II*, a spiral staircase to the sky lounge is lined with curved wood panels with a warm, glowing nickel-silver finish, inspired by a photograph of an ancient Roman mausoleum of Santa Costanza; the stair treads themselves are made of limestone. A glamorous bathroom on the *Aurora* has marble walls that are carved to look as if they were molded into soft curves. On the *Numptia*, one wall of the bar is a striking composition of panels made of alpaca (a metal alloy), in an *hommage* to the iconic pair of doors at the Villa Necchi Campiglio in Milan, a masterpiece of 1930s Rationalist architecture by Piero Portaluppi. And on the *Azimut 35*, Salvagni placed a writing desk directly in front of a large picture window—a location that is, as he says, "not what you'd expect." Sometimes, color is the means by which Salvagni surprises, as in his own apartment, where a wall of bright turquoise blue in the hallway from the foyer to the bedrooms serves as the backdrop for an elegant buffet by Osvaldo Borsani and a counterpoint to a pair of carved wood Tibetan doors beyond. Salvagni compares choices like this to adding an unusual ingredient to a conventional cocktail. "It's an element that doesn't fit the expected picture," he explains.

At other times, wit is the unexpected ingredient. "I love the idea of not being serious," Salvagni says. "I can wear a tailored suit, but then add pink socks, or I can add Yves Klein–blue cufflinks to a tuxedo" to create what he calls "dramatic conflict. Just using balanced pieces isn't effective." But Salvagni knows well that in audacity, as in many areas, moderation is the key; **DRAMA** just a subtle tweak can make all the difference, as when Salvagni took a nineteenth-century bust—a portrait of one of his mother's ancestors that stands in the winter garden of his apartment—and fitted it with a pair of goggles. In less-skilled hands, such a gesture might miss the mark, but for Salvagni, who knows the rules so well, breaking them in this case puts a lighthearted spin on history.

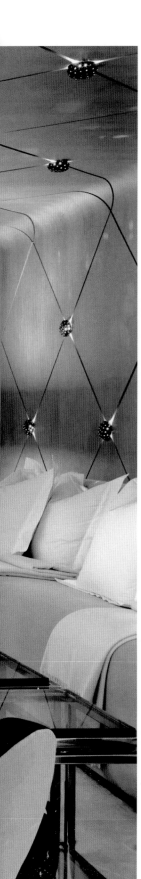

Villa Cimena near Turin by Renzo Mongiardino served as the inspiration for the seating area of the owner's suite of Numptia, which was designed to be distinctly elegant and calm.

"I don't design just for the sake of making something beautiful," Salvagni says. For him, one of the most important elements of design is contrast. "Real balance," he says, "is obtained through opposites. You need elements from very different places." In the same way, he says, his marriage is successful in part because he and his wife are each very different;

CONTRAST

in design, the contrasts between rough and smooth, straight and curvaceous, or rugged and soft can create the kind of tension that adds electricity. For instance, Salvagni points to his Saturn sconces, where the polished surface of the onyx contrasts with the rough texture of the cast bronze. "Imagine if they were both polished," he says. "It's the beauty of the extremes that creates the balance." Similarly, in a Fifth Avenue apartment, the spiky quality of a Pablo Avilla steel *Wire Tree* is offset by the lush contours of a magenta velvet chair Salvagni designed, as well as by the sensual curve of the bronze base of Hervé Van der Straeten's Substance side table, on which the tree sits.

The contrast between old and new offers another kind of tension. Salvagni has always been fascinated by the placement of contemporary art in a historic interior; he believes that "it makes it easier to appreciate the art." This is certainly true of his own apartment, where the moldings and pilasters of the late nineteenth-century architecture engage in a dialogue with the twentieth-century and contemporary painting and sculpture, or in the *Apollo* exhibition at Salvagni's London gallery, where the sleek, industrial quality of the "spaceship" wall contrasts with the tactile, artisanal quality of the furniture placed against it. The orchestration of these different tensions creates an emotional response—the "electricity" Salvagni mentions—to an object or a room.

Salvagni's earliest lesson in contrast occurred when he was a boy. He had envied the beige suede shoes he saw his friends wearing—"it was as if they belonged to a club," he recalls—so he was thrilled when his mother bought him a pair. But he quickly realized that everything about

THE ART OF THE MIX

the shoe was beige, so he substituted a pair of purple-red laces. The tension between the neutral tone of the shoe and the bright laces, he says, "created vibration vitality" and made his shoes truly his own, "not like everyone else's." Today, Salvagni's attention to this idea produces rooms that, like the shoes of his boyhood, do not look at all like everyone else's.

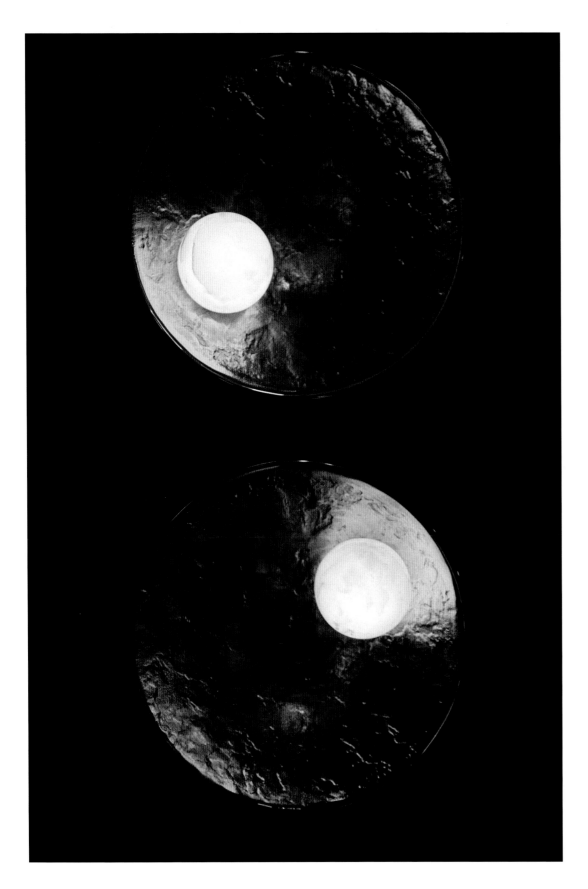

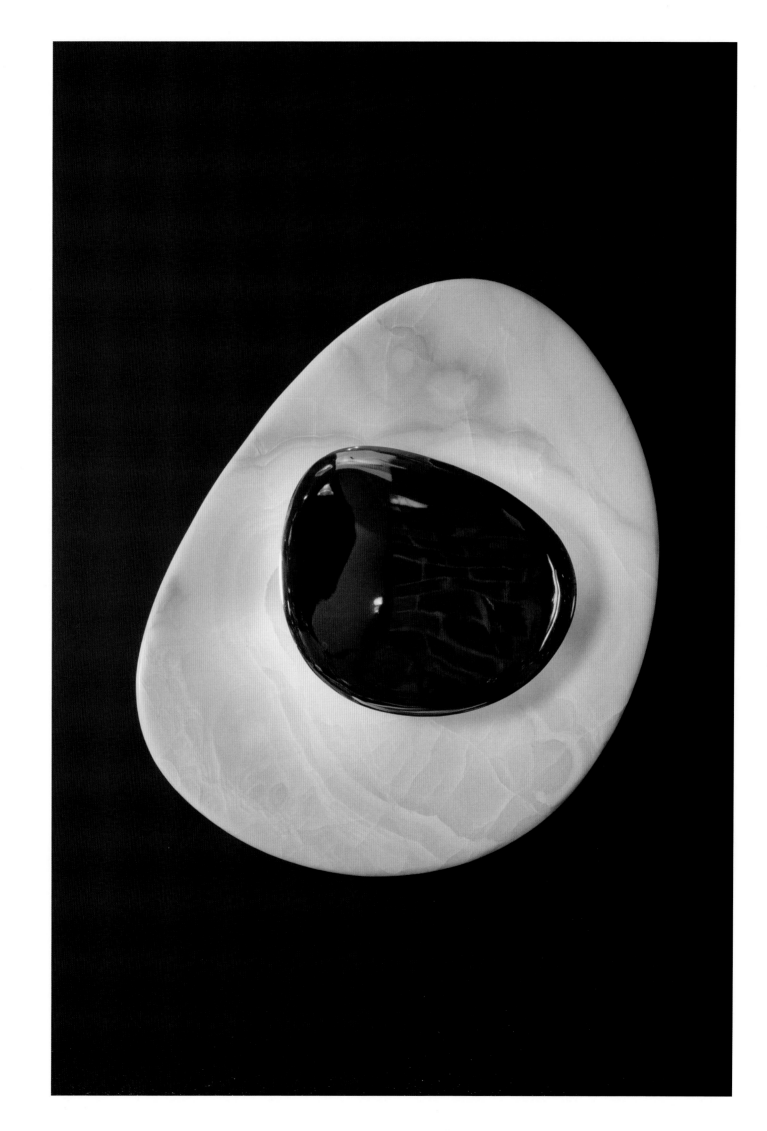

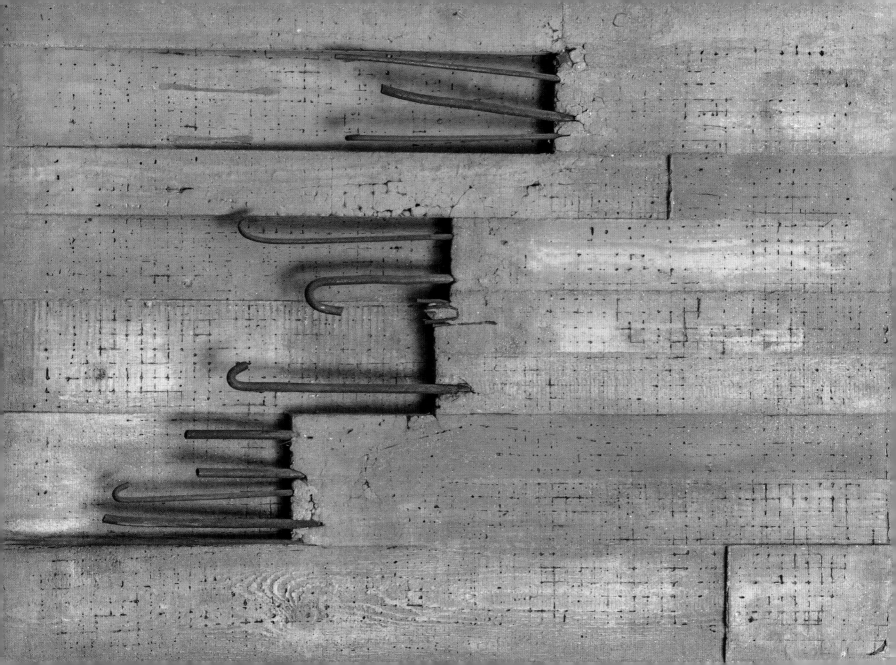

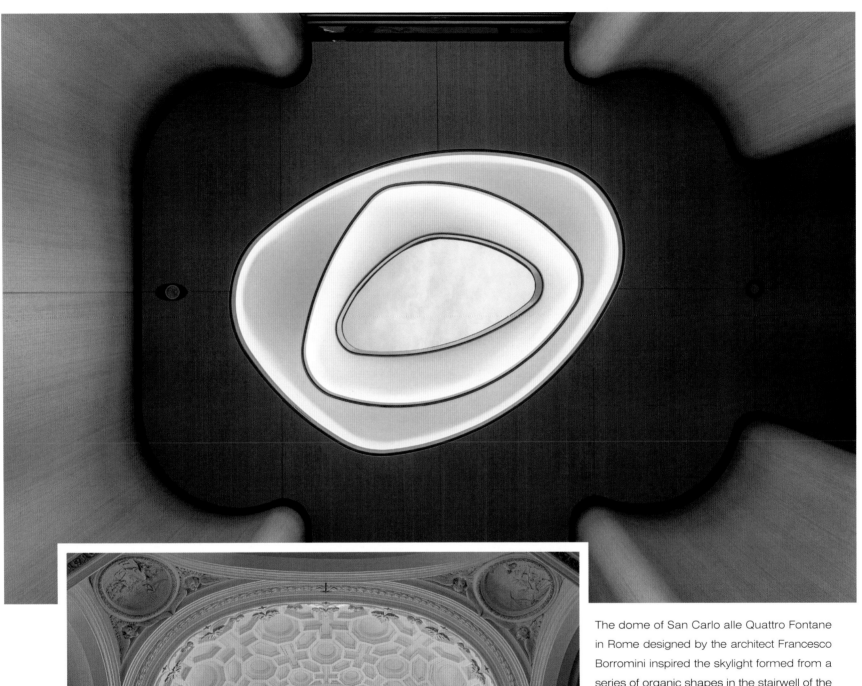

The dome of San Carlo alle Quattro Fontane in Rome designed by the architect Francesco Borromini inspired the skylight formed from a series of organic shapes in the stairwell of the superyacht *Aurora*.

The role of heritage—the legacy left to us by history—figures prominently in Salvagni's work. He grew up near Rome and attended university in the city. "I was exposed to a lot of art and architecture before I knew anything about it," he says. "It's something that really grows inside you." But while this immersion in history affected Salvagni deeply, his response **HERITAGE** as a designer has never been a literal one. He insists on the importance of knowing the past before attempting to look forward, but sees no point in trying to rehash it. Instead, he digests the lessons of the masters, then moves on. All great artists, architects, and designers, he says, "knew their past, but then went their own way."

When he designs, Salvagni immerses himself in the history of a place and its owners. In an apartment in the historic Palazzo Colonna in Rome, Salvagni designed the dining room around an ornate Venetian mirror, a family heirloom. The room's folding doors of wood, bronze, and silk open to frame a view of the mirror. In between, Salvagni designed a dining table that is a contemporary version of a marble table from the Roman Empire, which had vase-shaped supports. Salvagni's interpretation is made of limed royal oak, with the edge of the table top wrapped in a bronze "belt" that relates to both the doors and the gilt-wood mirror.

In the same vein, Salvagni's furniture and object designs express his deep knowledge of history in an emphatically modern vocabulary. He once lived in what had been a palace where Cesare and Lucrezia Borgia—both of whom were famous for poisoning their enemies—were born. Salvagni's Lancea lamp features a pointed dagger-like finial emerging from a perfectly detailed silk shade, expressing the idea of a "dark soul" appearing out of the seeming gentility of an "expensive dress." His Antinoo cabinet refers to Antinous, the beautiful Greek youth who was the lover of the Emperor Hadrian; Antinous's profile is outlined in gilt bronze between the cabinet's curved doors, which evoke Hadrian's possessive embrace. And in a more recent vein, Salvagni's famous Spider chandelier is inspired by

PROVENANCE & LEGACY a 1950s design by Angelo Lelli, an architect who founded the innovative lighting company Arredoluce. "I love the idea of a central 'mechanical' node with arms that move at different levels," Salvagni says, but while Lelli's light was industrially produced of metal and glass, Salvagni's version is made of bronze and onyx, using his own more sumptuous vocabulary of materials.

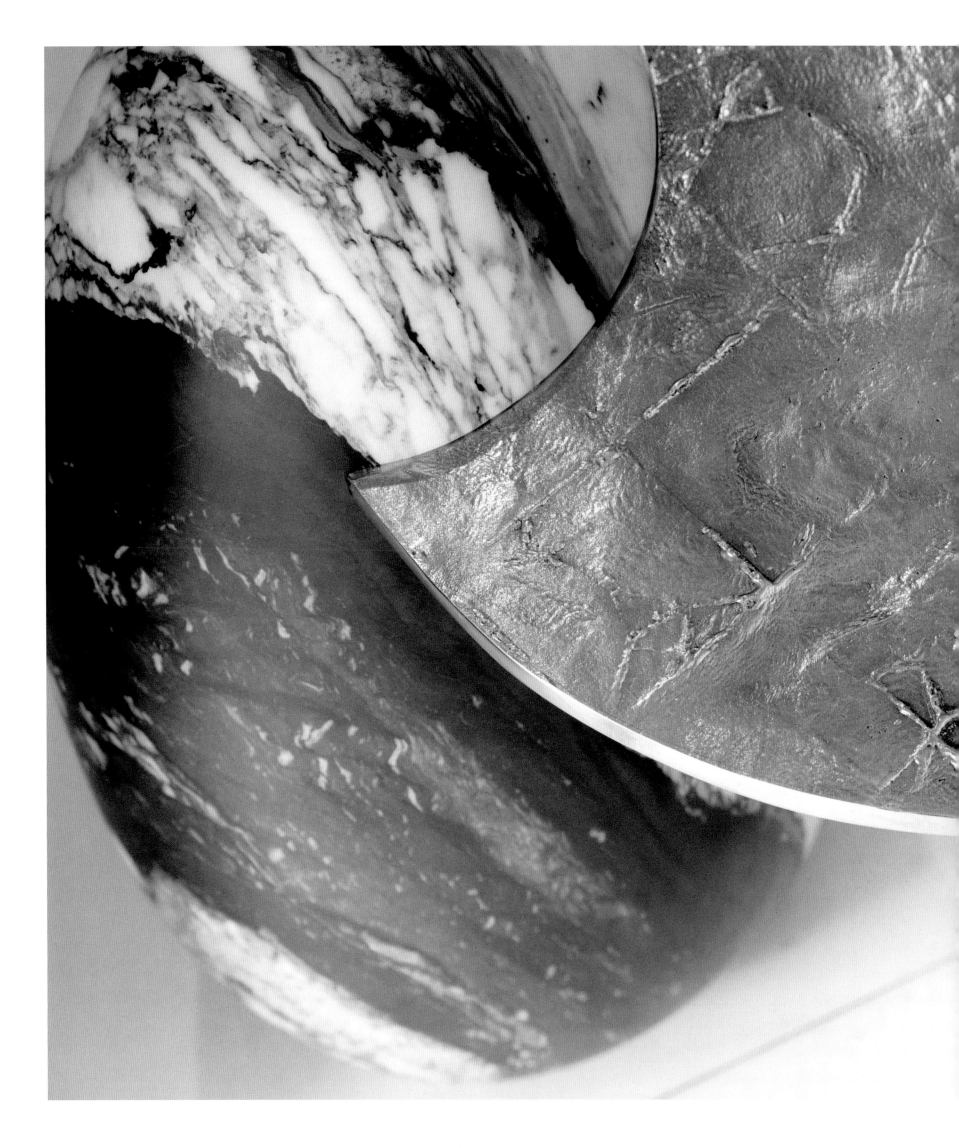

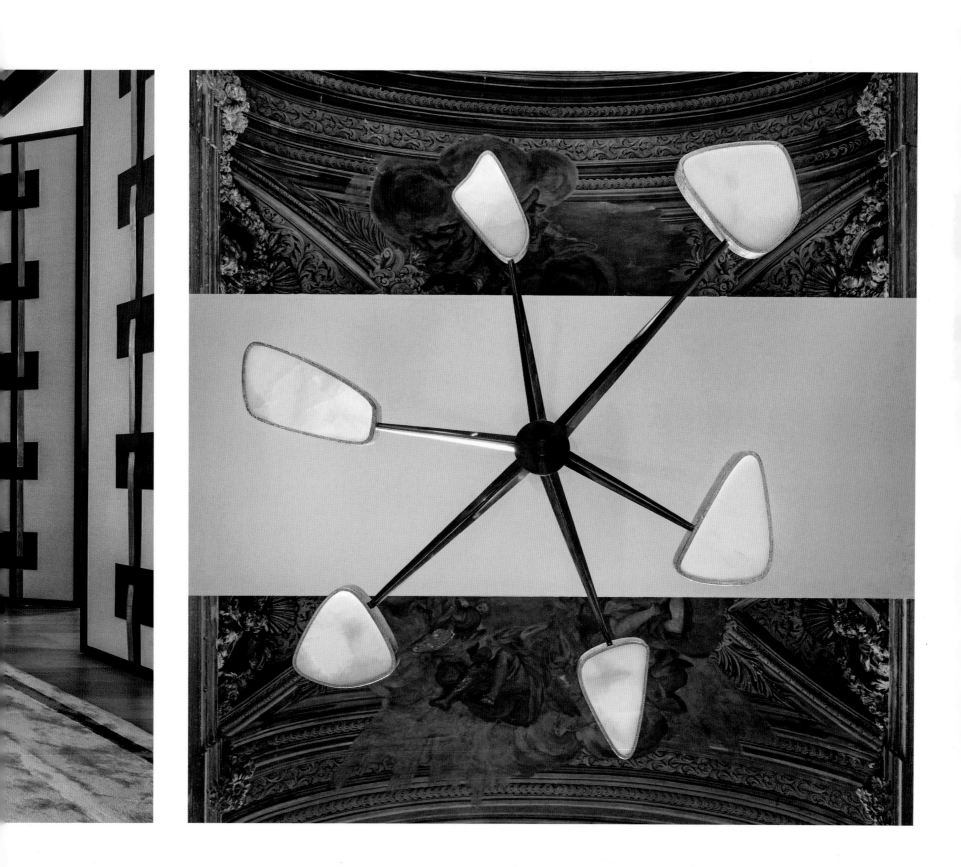

A detail of St. Peter's Square colonnades in Rome designed by Gian Lorenzo Bernini inspired this octagonal foyer that offers the first impression visitors have upon arrival to this Palm Beach oasis.

"I have always been fascinated by the idea of balance, and the harmony it produces," Salvagni says. A key component of balance is symmetry, but symmetry in the strictest sense doesn't always evoke the kind of emotional response that makes a room compelling. "I believe in *imperfect* symmetry—something that is not exactly mirrored," he explains, adding

BALANCE

that he is "much more interested in the accident than in the rule, because it's the accident that gives life to the rule." He notes that in nature, "the perfect balance always contains a small 'mistake.'" In Rome, a city full of Classical architecture, Salvagni is surrounded by symmetry, but he's constantly aware that it is the imperfect version that has the potential to be even more inspiring, by creating a feeling of balance, which is more about mood than it is about strict geometry. "Balance is mainly a state of mind rather than a physical scheme," he says.

In his interiors, Salvagni says he's "obsessed by the idea of focal points. A good space is a series of contrasts—of color, of fullness versus emptiness, of busy versus calm, or of presence versus absence." These focal points can take the form of an obvious disruption of symmetry, as in a Paris apartment where the clearly asymmetrical form of the living room fireplace, and the Salvagni-designed Clouds mirror that hangs above it, contrast with the matching chairs and symmetrical arrangements of framed prints on either side of the fireplace. At the entrance to the guest rooms on the yacht *Aurora*, the symmetry of the curved oak walls that frame Salvagni's Tango console is broken by the irregular, organic shape of the skylight above.

But the disruption can also be subtle, as with the dressing room of a Palm Beach apartment where the strict symmetry of the closet doors, made of wood with linen inserts, dominates the space—until you notice that the handles of the room's polished wooden doors—which are shaped like gingko leaves—are not identical. Similarly, the crystal "rays" that emanate from Salvagni's bronze and onyx Valentine sconce—a design named after his wife and inspired by an ex voto, or reli-

SYMMETRY

gious offering—are of unequal lengths, appearing slightly jagged in contrast to the more regular, tapering form of the sconce itself, reinforcing Salvagni's idea of creating something that "could have been perfect, but it's not." And it is this attention to imperfection—to the idea that constant perfection becomes monotonous—that creates a consistent sense of depth and surprise in Salvagni's work. His rooms are never out of balance, but they contain elements that inspire a second glance, making the experience even more memorable.

The fresco of the Tomb of the Diver, the archaeological site, informed the color palette and material choices for this London interior including a bespoke rug depicting the man diving in the waves.

For Salvagni, the idea of narrative in design is "the story behind the project, and I always have a story in mind," he says. That story is often a portrait of his client. "I don't start with a formal or aesthetic vision," he says. "I try to develop the idea based not on my own creativity," he continues, "but based on the client. I love that my design is the external expression of something." Salvagni talks to his clients, understands

NARRATIVE

who they are, and takes careful note of their histories and their interests, which inform his designs. For instance, when Salvagni was designing the interiors of the yacht *Endeavour II*, he realized that the owners' sensibilities were influenced by minimalism and Japanese art and design. "They like clean, clear, focused design," Salvagni explains. At a meeting, he noted that the wife of the couple was wearing tatami sandals, which influenced his design for floors made of panels wrapped in traditional tatami mats, custom made in Osaka, that Salvagni separated with burnished bronze inserts. "Elements like these become a wish list," Salvagni says. The *Endeavour II* also includes a curved wall in red lacquer, another reference to Japan, and a curved wall of reeded koto wood that evokes the slender stalks of bamboo; the shape of "floating" steps recalls the delicate petals of cherry blossoms. For an apartment in one of the oldest and grandest private palaces in Rome, Salvagni designed a rug woven with a map of the island where the owners spend every summer, and in the master bedroom, Salvagni alluded both to sixteenth-century Italian room dividers and to the abstracted Neoclassical architecture in Giorgio de Chirico's paintings in his design for a pair of arched doorways behind the bed that leads to a dressing room.

Narrative is also an essential part of the furniture and objects that Salvagni designs. "I could create portraits with my furniture," he says, "inspired by mythology, history, nature, and art." His Silk cabinet, with its sinuous wood doors—molded in the same way violins are made—evokes silk curtains billowing with the movement of air. The cabinet's gilt bronze hinges are like big jewels, Salvagni explains. "It's

STORYTELLING

a Baroque approach," he says. "It's overdressed." The angular, asymmetrical bronze base of the Tango cabinet was inspired by a visit to Buenos Aires, where he was fascinated by the movement of dancers' legs. "Much of the time, their feet slide," he says, "so the base of the console traces those patterns. And the twisted forms of the legs refer to the dancers' bodies." For Salvagni, every room, every object, tells a story.

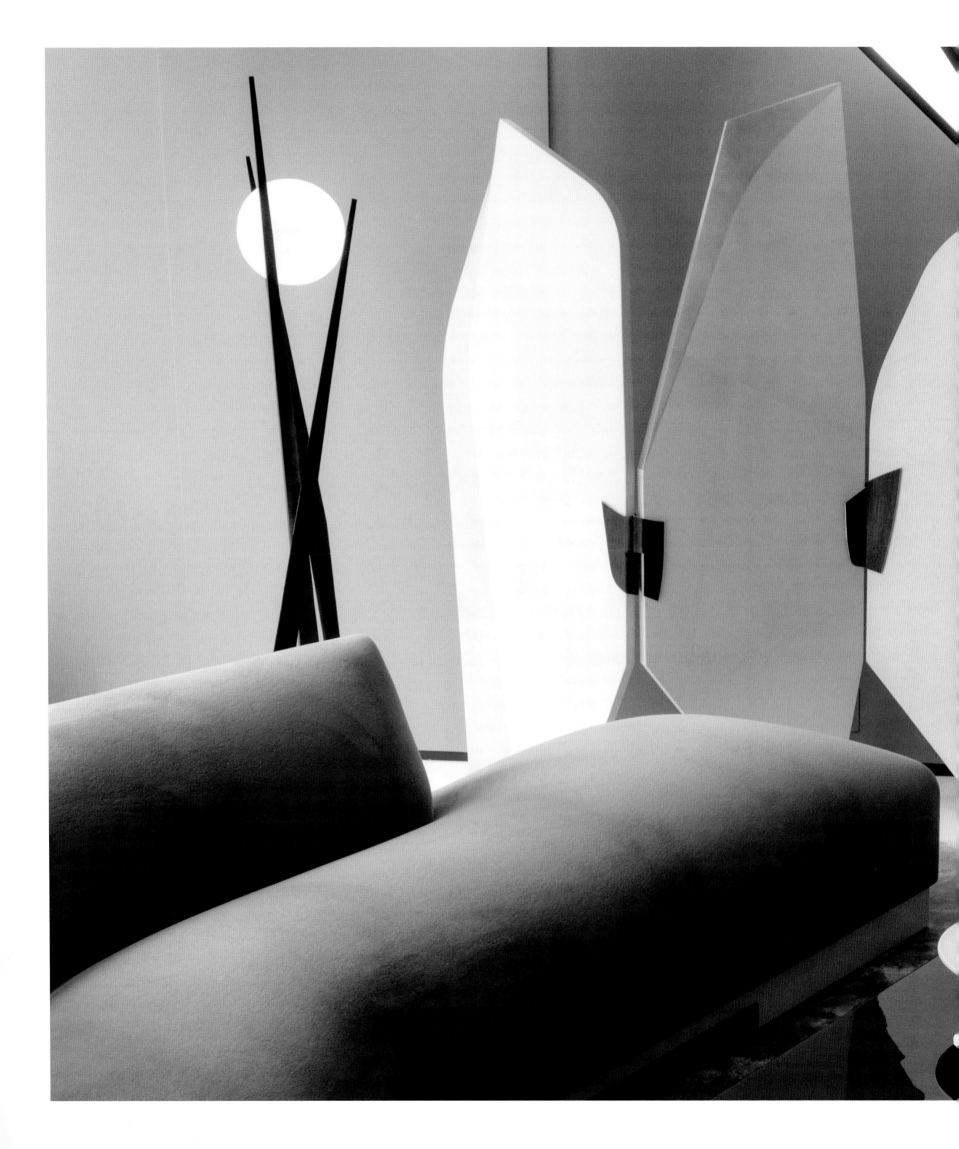

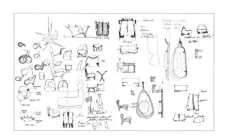

FRONT ENDPAPER Conceptual sketches by Achille Salvagni.

BACK OF FRONT ENDPAPER Kenya's safari camps served as the design inspiration for Salvagni's Amboseli armchair. This modern interpretation is made of walnut and features cast bronze details.

P. 6 Illustration of the architect and designer Achille Salvagni surrounded by his own designs drawn by Jean-Philippe Delhomme.

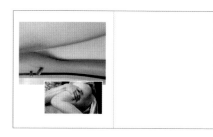

P. 14 The curves of Gian Lorenzo Bernini's *The Rape of Proserpina* inform Salvagni's sculptural approach to designing yacht interiors. Here, wood with bronze inlay, lacquered fiberglass, and leather over fiberglass cover up mechanical equipment and beams in the ceiling of an Azimut Grande twenty-seven-meter yacht.

P. 16–17 The main stairwell of the superyacht *Endeavour II* is made from parchment-dressed fiberglass and polished German silver and is inspired by the neutral sophistication of Japanese design.

P. 18–19 A fireplace with an undulating curved design made of parchment, Sahara noir marble, and polished brass is coupled with a pair of gently bowed bronze andirons.

P. 20–21 Living room featuring a sinuous curved sofa onboard an Azimut thirty-five meter yacht. **P. 21** Salvagni's organically shaped cabinet in a room with limited space provides storage and adds visual interest.

P. 22–23 This "growing lamp" is part of the cabinet; it evokes the softness of a natural growing branch and connects the lamp to the cabinet, preventing it from sliding off.

P. 24–25 A limited-edition Drop side table with a twenty-four-carat gold leaf top and bronze legs with two types of finishes is paired with a Papillia armchair with tufted blue velvet upholstery.

P. 26–27 A nightstand with a free-floating design integrates into the headboard, wrapping and bending to create volume on this Azimut yacht—warmth meant for a bedroom but with the design and function for a yacht.

P. 28–29 The sculptural details of the superyacht *Aurora*: in the hallway and the closet doors of the owner's suite, Salvagni provided a curtain effect.

P. 30–31 Leros, a light sculpture with hand-carved onyx demispheres and polished bronze rope, is named for the Greek island. Composed of four islets, the inclusive perimeter references the island's shape.

P. 32–33 Vittoria armchairs, featuring velvet upholstery and a metallic lacquered base, flank Cosmedin, an egg-shaped marble block side table with a cast aluminum shelf. **P. 33** Angel and Devil mirrors (Aldus collection) rest on a Silk Gold cabinet.

P. 34–35 Detail from the front of Palatino, a two-door cabinet clad in parchment, topped in bronze, with Rosso Levanto marble decoration and custom hinges.

P. 36–37 The sitting room in the master bedroom suite on board the superyacht *Numptia* features a mix of bespoke and antique furniture to create a home on the sea.

P. 38–39 One of the guest cabins on an Azimut twenty-seven-meter yacht features soft clean lines and a neutral palette designed to create a sense of warmth and wellness.

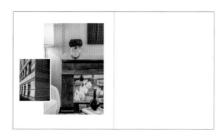

P. 41 Moon candlesticks from the Aldus collection on top of the Diomede console. On the wall is Valentine, an organically shaped mirror made of hand-hammered twenty-four-carat gold plated polished bronze with mirrored glass and crystal shards.

P. 42 Salvagni's inspiration for the shape of the fireplace in a New York pied-à-terre is from the architecture of the Rosario Candela–designed building at 19 East 76th Street in Manhattan.

P. 44–45 Contemporary living room in Geneva features a parchment fireplace surround flanked by a pair of Pillow Magnum sconces, Ares coffee table, and Amboseli chairs on top of a green silk rug.

P. 46 Alternating strips of Carrara and Belgian marble define the kitchen in Salavgni's Rome residence. **P. 46–47** The arm of a green upholstered Salvagni sofa from the Gio Collection, paired with Salvagni's Hercules lamp and Simposio chandelier in a London interior.

P. 48–49 Juxtaposing lavish fabrics with highly lacquered bases demonstrates the importance of surface and material in Salvagni's work. Pietra, a table in polished walnut, sits in front of Garda, with its high pile wool and yellow lacquered base.

P. 50–51 Japan informed this London interior, where Oyster wall sconces bring warmth to the space with polished bronze, backlit hand-carved onyx radiates light, and the Gae armchair references Isamu Noguchi and Isamu Kenmochi's basket chair.

P. 52–53 A selection of Achille Salvagni Atelier limited-edition furniture and lighting in signature materials including bronze, onyx, and glossy lacquers at the Pavilion of Art + Design in Geneva.

P. 54–55 Three multifaceted Emerald side tables each in a different finish work well together paired with a modern sofa. **P. 55** The master suite of the superyacht *Endeavour II* features an Emerald side table with a Nino Zoncada chair.

P. 56–57 A fresco from the House of Augustus in Rome depicting the ancient city of Pompeii inspired this London interior, where Salvagni brought together materials including marble, bronze, and walnut to create stunning pieces with historical references.

P. 58–59 A lounge area with soft, soothing, warm tones and textures on the top deck of the superyacht *Endeavour II*.

P. 60 The living room of a Palm Beach residence that features a balance of soft shades punctuated with vivid colors such as on the base of this bespoke coffee table.

P. 62 Above a Paolo Buffa bar cabinet hangs an artwork by Giuseppe Uncini in the colorful living room of Salvagni's Rome residence. **P. 62–63** The Osaka desk handcrafted from lacewood features a pair of built-in reading lights with bronze inlays engraved on the surface of the desk. This pattern is picked up and reflected on the doors of the Palatino cabinet.

P. 64 The sunshine-yellow upholstered Tato armchair is named for Guglielmo Tato Sansoni, a proponent of the futurist movement. The artwork in the background is by Lucio Fontana. **P. 65** Parchment with handcrafted bronze elements is a common pairing for Salvagni—seen here in the Perseo vase from the Aldus collection and with the Circeo screen.

P. 66–67 Plush curvilinear furniture, floor to ceiling windows, and chic color schemes are among the features in this living room designed for entertaining and relaxing in luxury on board an Azimut thirty-five-meter yacht.

P. 68–69 A work by Anish Kapoor hangs on the undulating walls made of velvet textured limed oak to create a cocoonlike feeling inside the superyacht *Aurora*. **P. 69** The Palatino cabinet is shown against a red painted wall at the Pavilion of Art + Design in Geneva.

P. 71 The upstairs hallway in the private quarters of an estate in Southampton, New York features a soft color palette, twentieth-century design, and items from the client's art collection.

P. 72–73 A collection of limited-edition works by Achille Salvagni Atelier in a London interior includes Earring sconces, Vittoria armchairs, a Drop side table, and a Nemo lamp.

P. 74 A fresco by Raffaellino del Colle representing Saint Leo the Great from Oratorio di San Leo in Sansepolcro inspired the base of Salvagni's Roma cabinet. Each cast bronze leg is shaped like the pope's tiara.

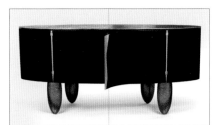

P. 76–77 Roma is a double-door cabinet made in European walnut with cast bronze details. Rome is the inspiration, including the city's ellipse shape and sense of mystery, which is expressed in the cabinet's closed doors.

P. 78–79 Salvagni's craftsmen are the same generations of tradesmen that have taken care of restoring the bronze works at the Vatican and papal residences for centuries. **P. 79** Inspired by a trip to Buenos Aires, the Tango console's structure references the legs of dancers, as they intertwine and cross over one another.

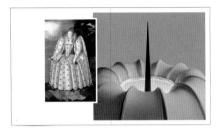

P. 80–81 The "Ditchley portrait" of Queen Elizabeth I by Marcus Gheeraerts the Younger informed the shape of the handmade and stitched Japanese silk lampshade that adorns the Lancea lamps and was created by an eighty-five-year-old woman who was formerly the assistant of Renzo Mongiardino.

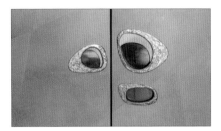

P. 82–83 The Nerone cocktail cabinet was named for the demigod Roman emperor who was killed by a stab to the heart. The red lacquer on the handle represents blood from the wound that resulted in his demise.

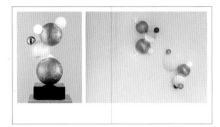

P. 84 The Bubbles table lamp was created as a bespoke piece inspired by the work of Jeff Koons, referencing his playful approach to depicting animated figures. **P. 84–85** . Bubbles sconces are a new spin on the original lighting design.

P. 86–87 Salvagni works with cloistered nuns known for their embroidery to create the textiles that line the interior of many Aldus pieces including the Aldus symbol, the snail and the rabbit, being sewn here.

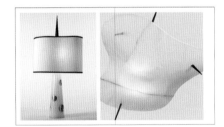

P. 88–89 The designs for the Nemo table lamp and the Darts chandelier demonstrate Salvagni's penchant for using exceptional materials such as the cool luminous, onyx and patinated bronze in extraordinary ways.

P. 90–91 The top lounge on the superyacht *Endeavour II*: the curve of the walls and the soft organic shapes of the cabinet and attached lamp are all meant to maintain a serene, natural, balanced atmosphere.

P. 92–93 A limited-edition Tango console made with a white parchment top contrasts with dark patinated bronze legs.

P. 94–95 Antinous, the beautiful Greek youth believed to be the secret lover of the Roman Emperor Hadrian, inspired the cabinet of the same name. This relationship is represented in a subtle face on the bronze panel in the center of the credenza's two doors.

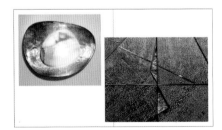

P. 96–97 The Oyster wall sconce features polished bronze and backlit hand-carved onyx that gently radiates light and a detail of the cast bronze handles on the Gio Lacewood cabinet.

P. 98–99 Detail of Diomede, a cast-bronze console table with a marble top, is a fitting homage to the mythical Greek hero of the Trojan War and his golden armor.

P. 100–101 Moon candlesticks from the Aldus collection sit on top of the richly colored marble top of the cast-bronze Diomede console table.

P. 102–103 Pietra, an asymmetrical multifaceted coffee table in French polished walnut, takes its name from the Italian word for "rock." **P. 103** The Lucy mirror, named after the first human ancestor found in Ethiopia, and the stone shape refer to the tools used by our primitive ancestors.

P. 104–105 Craftsmen use the same construction techniques that they have since the seventeenth century to make the body of violins to create Silk Gold cabinet. Salvagni works with Roman artisans renowned for their traditional techniques in the Vatican City and among the cabinet-makers of the Quirinal Palace.

P. 106–107 The Silk Gold cabinet is finished to gilded perfection with sinuous curves and a handle inlaid with onyx, giving it the right balance of sophistication and glamour.

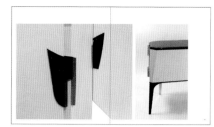

P. 108–109 Bronze hinges on the parchment panels of the Circeo screen, named for Monte Circeo, the sandstone formations dating from the Jurassic period. P. 109 The Antinoo cabinet is finished in white parchment with gilt bronze hinges and patinated-bronze legs.

P. 111 Simposio, a chandelier with a staggered succession of three vertically arranged patinated-bronze bowls.

P. 112 The influence of the mosaics in the adulatory vault Santa Costanza Church in Rome can be seen in the staircase of this Rossinavi superyacht, including the curved wooden panels with a metallic-looking finish.

P. 114–115 Sinuous curves, dramatic backdrops, hand-polished finishes, luxurious materials such as bronze and onyx, and art from the Spatialism movement are hallmarks of Salvagni's designs.

P. 116–117 The distinctively dark painted hallway distinguishes and separates the public spaces from the private ones in Salvagni's Rome residence. P. 117 A selection of works highlights the range of unexpected materials and lush finishes at Maison Gerard in New York.

P. 118–119 Chaos, a small bronze vase from the Aldus collection, and the organically shaped mirror Squiggles finished with two types of brass.

P. 120–121 Gentle radial curves and neutral colors create the calming atmosphere found in the sitting room on the top deck of the superyacht Endeavour II.

P. 122–123 Salvagni transformed this interior in Mayfair into a retro-futuristic space capsule inspired by set designs from iconic 1960s science-fiction films.

P. 124 A vintage console sits under the television in Salvagni's Rome residence. P. 124–125 A custom-designed one is placed in front of the large floor to ceiling window on an Azimut thirty-five-meter yacht.

P. 126–127 To create the lush allure of this Parisian bedroom, Salvagni used soft shapes, as he believes their sensuality helps to stimulate the senses. P. 127 Clean lines and soft tones keep this busy corridor in balance.

P. 128–129 A bedroom inside a Palm Beach residence featuring bespoke furniture gives this interior its 1950s and 1960s Italian panache, reminiscent of the work of Gio Ponti and Paolo Buffa.

P. 130–131 A bathroom aboard the superyacht Aurora where Salvagni infused the interiors of the incredible vessel with a host of luxurious materials including Calacatta marble and dark polished ebony walls.

P. 132 The winter garden's plaster bust, circa 1830, with swimming goggles inside Salvagni's Rome apartment.

P. 135–136 Looking up the main staircase at a series of custom circular mirrors and the organically shaped skylight on the top floor inside a town house in London's prestigious Holland Park.

P. 136–137 Beautiful detail of the curved limed oak and red lacquer wall outside the guest cabin of the superyacht *Endeavour II*.

P. 138–139 The kitchen in Salvagni's Rome residence features an island in Absolute Black Marble, cabinetry by Poggenpohl, and a nineteenth-century oil on canvas portrait of a family member.

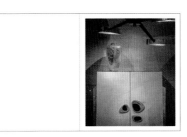

P. 141 Nerone, a double-door bar cabinet in parchment-lined walnut with Sahara Noir marble and glass shelves. It mounts twenty-four-carat gold-plated cast bronze hinges and cutout handles in cast bronze with red lacquered details.

P. 142–143 The main saloon of *Numptia*, a 230-foot superyacht, features a cathedral-style ceiling in teak with curved walls and lights that represent sea urchins. **P. 143** Soft forms and organic shapes pair with artifacts, sculpture, and distinctive furniture.

P. 144–145 Pompeii was the inspiration for this London interior featuring textures of shattered stone, marble, and an opulent color palette.

P. 146 The Villa Cimena near Turin by Renzo Mongiardino served as the inspiration for the seating area of the owner's suite of *Numptia*, which was designed to be distinctly elegant and calm.

P. 148–149 The natural beauty outside this Fifth Avenue residence complements the textures and shapes inside, accented by red leather chairs by Jacques Adnet, an ebony games table, a Fontana Arte side table, and a Nemo table lamp designed by Salvagni.

P. 150–151 Salvagni brings together rich and varied textures, from delicate finishes to polished woods and bronzes to smooth mineral stones, in Antinoo and the Soitrio table lamp Tango with Nilo centerpiece.

P. 152–153 The living room inside a Rive Gauche Parisian residence incorporates a mix of works designed by Salvagni and important twentieth-century design to reflect the rich sense of history found in this Île-de-France neighborhood.

P. 154–155 Bronze Saturn sconces are illuminated by a celestial onyx sphere, reminiscent of a satellite in orbit. *Endeavour II*, a 170-foot superyacht, is a study in restrained elegance and sophistication, with materials including bronze, limed oak, and tatami wood.

P. 156–157 The cast bronze hand-engraved feet of Salvagni's Gae chair are paired with a Gio Ponti walnut and brass wall bench originally produced for the Palazzo Contini Bonacossi in Florence.

P. 158–159 Salvagni's classic editions at Maison Gerard in New York include an Elena chandelier hanging above a Palatino cabinet with ornamental lapis lazuli marble details and an Oyster mirror set in a veined, slightly concave piece of onyx.

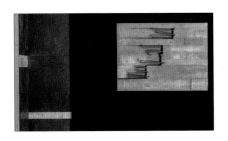

P. 160–161 An artwork in Salvagni's own collection by Giuseppe Uncini.

P. 162 The design of Tato references art deco and 1930s industrial design.
P. 162–163 Salvagni brings together the Osaka desk and Palatino cabinet with a Valentine Mirror Magnum, named for his wife, Valentina, and a photograph by Vanessa Beecroft.

P. 164–165 Salvagni's bedroom in his Rome residence, where his extensive art collection is on view and paired with a bespoke cabinet of his design.

P. 166 For a living room in Geneva, Salvagni pairs a table by Paolo Buffa with four limited-edition Frangipane chairs and a Lens chandelier that casts a soft glow to view artwork by Jacob Kassay.

P. 168–169 Two curved love seats designed by Salvagni allude to the Sahara's sand dunes, while the fire orange color of the upholstery is reminiscent of the sunset.

P. 170–171 Salvagni's Rome residence has a soft, natural color palette inspired by Old Master paintings, inherited pieces, and investment art. P. 171 He mixes different periods with items from auctions, flea markets, galleries, and antiques shops alongside his own designs.

P. 172–173 For a guest bedroom in a Left Bank pied-à-terre, Salvagni created a sense of comfort and security through his selection of lush materials and soft shapes.

P. 174–175 A bathroom in Salvagni's Rome residence features a dramatic color palette of ultramarine, sienna, ocher, and umber. A series of ancient battle scene etchings hangs over the tub, creating a classical element within this space.

P. 177 The living room in a New York pied-à-terre features luxurious materials, rich colors, and organic shapes.

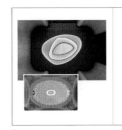

P. 178 The dome of San Carlo alle Quattro Fontane in Rome designed by the architect Francesco Borromini inspired the skylight formed from a series of organic shapes in the stairwell of the superyacht Aurora.

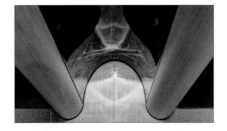

P. 180–181 The curved limed oak and red lacquered wall featured on the superyacht Endeavour II.

P. 182–183 Detail from the huge limestone bas-relief depicting a tropical scene that hangs in the main dining room of the superyacht Numptia. Salvagni designed this space to be about emotion and style.

P. 184–185 At the Pavilion of Art + Design London, Salvagni presented an ocher-tinged "Sahara" showcase—a series of desert-inspired limited-edition pieces.

P. 187 An Aracne picture frame in glass and cast bronze from the Aldus collection.

P. 188–189 The main stairwell of the superyacht Endeavour II is made of limestone and polished nickel.

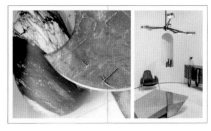

P. 190–191 Natural materials and artisan details exemplify Salvagni's work: the Cosmedin side table, the iconic Spider chandelier in patinated bronze and onyx, the Papillia armchair, the Pietra coffee table in alpaca and lacewood, and the Roma cabinet.

P. 192–193 The living room in Salvagni's Rome residence demonstrates the designer's appreciation for color and his ability to blend a variety of tones, textiles, and shapes in playful and engaging ways.

P. 194–195 One of the well-appointed guest cabins on the superyacht Endeavour II features a custom light and a wenge wood chair.

P. 196–197 Salvagni transformed a dining room inside a Roman palazzo by mixing family heirlooms with contemporary Italian designs. P. 197 A Spider chandelier hanging in Sant'Angelo in Pescheria, an eighth-century church built on the ruins of the ancient Porticus Octaviae.

P. 198–199 The master area corridor in a Palm Beach residence features custom door handles from the Aldus collection and a carved and limed wood male torso after the antique, circa 1940, on a black Zimbabwe marble base.

P. 200–201 The master bedroom in a New York pied-à-terre echoes a Piet Mondrian painting with blocks of color. **P. 201** A pair of carved Rosso Levanto marble Dolmen candlestick holders against a teal backdrop.

P. 202 A detail of Saint Peter's Square colonnades in Rome designed by Gian Lorenzo Bernini inspired this octagonal foyer that offers the first impression visitors have upon arrival at this Palm Beach oasis.

P. 204–205 The main living room on the superyacht *Endeavour II* features a tatami wood floor with bronze inlay, custom seating, and original 1960s Stila Nova floor lamps.

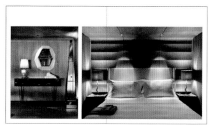

P. 206 A harmonious blend of luxury with calming ambience is the atmosphere Salvagni created on the superyacht *Numptia*. **P. 206–207** A guest room provides a comforting sensation of being cocooned within the space.

P. 208–209 The grand teak curved staircase on the superyacht *Numptia*.

P. 210–211 In Salvagni's Rome living room, a Louis XV console sits underneath a painting by Ettore Spalletti, *Una giornata di sole e oro* (2011), and Nino Zoncada's armchairs beneath Ilya and Emilia Kabakov's oil on canvas.

P. 212–213 The seating area within the owner's cabin on board a thirty-two-meter Azimut yacht features custom furniture and lighting.

P. 214–215 Salvagni's muse for this New York interior was his client who dresses in neutral tones with punches of color. He translated this into the living room with persimmon pillows and pops of red in the artwork.

P. 216–217 For a Parisian living room in a historic building located in the 6th arrondissement, Salvagni created a refined interior with muted colors, combining organic forms with precious materials and juxtaposing styles in a contemporary way.

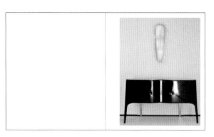

P. 219 A limited-edition Antinoo cabinet in polished walnut sits underneath the glow of a Valentina Magnum mirror.

P. 220–221 A den in a New York residence features a white oak wall with a richly textured finish and a zebra pouf designed by Salvagni to give it a sense of drama and glamour.

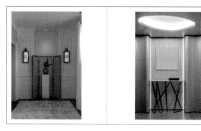

P. 222–223 Color, shape, and softness transform two hallways: a Southampton, New york, estate features a frothy palette like those along the Amalfi Coast in the 1940s and 1950s and *Aurora* with soft curves, limed sycamore walls, and contemporary artwork.

P. 224–225 An oval dining room in Rome features vintage Warren Platner dining chairs with a custom round table, a black lacquered spider chandelier, and onyx wall details. Bronze archways add a touch of glamour.

P. 226–227 Entrance to the private quarters of an apartment inside the Palazzo Colonna in Rome. The walls are upholstered in silk and the doors covered in Ultrasuede accented with nailheads.

P. 228–229 Details from an apartment inside the Palazzo Colonna in Rome: a hallway with a custom bench and family portrait and a living room with a stately fireplace made of Noir Saint Laurent.

P. 230–231 A dining room in a nineteenth-century town house in Holland Park, London, features an Enrico Castellani painting and vintage 1950s Italian dining chairs, along with a bespoke chandelier, parchment cabinet, and silk knotted carpet.

P. 232–233 A green-toned study in a London interior features a pair of San Lorenzo bookshelves and an Elana ceiling pendant made of shards of onyx and bronze.

P. 234–235 With an emphasis on the details, Salvagni carefully curated this family den in a Southampton, New York, estate with a mix of periods and styles, adding playful touches of color and gold accents.

P. 237 The colors of the Almalfi Coast popular in the 1940s and 1950s inspired this blue master bathroom that features a pale carved-marble tub, a nod to the ancient Roman bath, in this Southampton, New York, estate.

P. 238–239 The gallery in a Southampton, New York, estate features a double-height ceiling and is furnished with bespoke works including a special version of Silk, made of royal oak with a cast bronze top.

P. 240 The fresco of the Tomb of the Diver, the archaeological site, informed the color palette and material choices for this London interior including a bespoke rug depicting the man diving in the waves.

P. 242–243 Salvagni placed 1950s red leather lounge chairs by Jacques Adnet and an ebony games table against the window to take advantage of the light and views in this Fifth Avenue apartment.

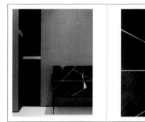

P. 244–245 Giò pays homage to Salvagni's predecessor, Gio Ponti. The cabinet possesses elements of the earlier artist's aesthetic, which have been adapted into a design all Salvagni's own.

P. 246–247 Lutece, Salvagni's collection for JL Coquet, is a take on the iconic Hemispheres design. Inspired by the ancient civilizations of Rome and Lutetia, drawing on the original, he reinvigorated it with his signature style.

P. 248–249 The door in the master bedroom suite in Palm Beach is lacquered and features a custom bronze door handle from the Aldus collection.

P. 250–251 The saloon of the superyacht *Numptia* features soft forms and organic shapes paired with natural elements and textures. All the pieces are bespoke, drawing inspiration from Italian design from the 1930s to the 1950s.

P. 252–253 In this London interior, Salvagni balances creamy neutrals and bold colors perfectly, pairing Circeo, a parchment screen, and the Divo floor lamp with the vividly upholstered Garda sofa in green Dedar fabric.

P. 254–255 A Parisian pied-à-terre features a mix of pieces designed by Salvagni and important twentieth-century works to reflect the rich sense of history found in this Île-de-France neighborhood.

P. 256–257 The Ebe mirror in Rosso Levanto marble with a polished and protected cast bronze frame. **P. 257** Custom His-and-Her twenty-four-carat gold plated door handles from the Aldus collection.

P. 258–259 Bronze, a favored material of Salvagni, takes on many forms and finishes from the Chaos vase to the Gae chair with cast-bronze hand-engraved feet to the Silk Gold cabinet to the Darts chandelier.

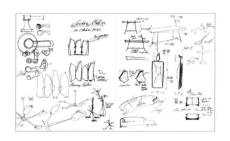

P. 260 The hallway outside Salvagni's distinctive kitchen with its black-and-white striped marble flooring in his Rome residence. **P. 261** Cosmedin, an egg-shaped hand-carved marble block side table with cast aluminum shelf.

BACK ENDPAPER Conceptual sketches by Achille Salvagni.

Thanks to my wife, Valentina, who is a constant source of inspiration, and my children Gaetano and Vittoria, whose energy and joy offer me a fresh perspective. I hope that this book will one day help them better understand my

ACKNOWLEDGMENTS

work. Thanks to Dad and Mom, for always supporting me throughout childhood and my career, and to my sister Marcella, for accepting me for who I am. Thanks to Benoist F. Drut for believing in me from the very beginning. A special thanks to Riccardo Sanchini for his loyal friendship and his support ever since university, and to Fabio Gnessi for his "Aldus" approach to life. And to Paolo Petrignani, whose photographs transcend art. Thanks to Marco Curi and Jacopo Belloni for their inherent passion and devotion. Thanks to my team in Rome, in alphabetical order: Marco Di Giovanni, Antonio Langone, Antonella Mantovani, Francesca Mazzuca, Andrea Pasquini, Daniela Ricci, Gabriele Scorza, Tanit Sindin, and Daniele Tummolo; and to my London team: Attilio Foa, James Malcolm Green, and Laure

ACHILLE SALVAGNI

Rouge with the support of Daniele Reiber. And special thanks to Stacy McLaughlin and Pilar Viladas, without whose efforts this book would not have been possible, not to mention the contributions of Sam Shahid and Matt Kraus. I truly appreciate their time and wisdom—as well as that of Dung Ngo and the Rizzoli team. I would also like to thank Marco and Paolo for their superb craftsmanship which fully embodies the refinement of my work.

PHOTOGRAPHY AND ILLUSTRATION CREDITS

JEAN-PHILIPPE DELHOMME: case cover, 6; ACHILLE SALVAGNI: front endpaper; PAOLO PETRIGNANI: pp. 14, 16–17, 20-21, 22- 23, 24–25, 26–27, 28–29, 30–31, 32-33, 38–39, 42, 46, 46–47, 50-51, 55, 56–57, 58–59, 60, 62, 65, 66–67, 68–69, 71, 78–79, 84–85, 86–87, 98–99, 100-101, 104–5, 112, 114–15, 116–17, 118–19, 120–21, 122–23, 124, 124–25, 126–27, 127, 128–29, 130-31, 132, 134–35, 136–37, 138–39, 141, 144-45, 148–49, 150-51, 152-53, 154-55, 156–57, 160-61, 162-163, 164–65, 166, 168–69, 170-71, 172–73, 174, 177, 178, 180–81, 184-85 187, 188–89, 190–91, 191, 192–93, 194–95, 196-97, 198–99, 200–201, 202, 204–5, 210–11, 212-13, 214-15, 216–17, 220–21, 222, 223, 224–25, 226–27, 228–29, 229, 230–31, 232–33, 234-35, 237, 238–39, 240, 242–43, 246–47, 248–49, 252–53, 254–55, 256–57, 257, 260; PHILIPPE KLIOT: cover, pp. 18-19, 64, 79, 90–91, 154, 201; JEAN FRANCOIS JAUSSARD: pp. 33, 117, 158, 159, 259; MARIS MEZULIS: pp. 34–35, 41, 44–45, 52-53, 62-63, 69, 166; MASSIMO LISTRI: pp. 36-37, 142–43, 143, 146, 182-83, 206, 206–207, 208-09, 250-251; JAMES MACDONALD: pp. 54-55, 72–73, 92–93, 219, 244-45; ACHILLE SALVAGNI ATELIER: back of endpapers, pp. 14 (inset), 42 (inset), 57(inset), 74, 76–77, 79, 80-81, 82-83, 84, 88, 88–89, 94-95, 96-97, 102-03, 106–07, 108–09, 111, 178 (inset), 202 (inset) 258, 261; ARIAN CAMILLERI: p. 151; INSTITUZIONE CULTURALE MUSEO CIVICO DI SAN SEPOLCRO: p.74 (inset); NATIONAL PORTRAIT GALLERY, LONDRES: p. 80 (inset); NATIONAL GEOGRAPHIC: p. 95 (inset); LUCA PARRA-VANO: p. 112; MARIO CIAMPI: p. 146 (inset); PUBLIC DOMAIN: p. 240 (inset)

First published in the United States of America in 2019 by
Rizzoli International Publications, Inc.
300 Park Avenue South
New York, NY 10010
www.rizzoliusa.com

Copyright © 2019 Achille Salvagni
Text: Pilar Viladas

Publisher: Charles Miers
Editor: Dung Ngo
Design by Sam Shahid
Art Director: Matthew Kraus
Production Manager: Kaija Markoe
Managing Editor: Lynn Scrabis

Printed in China

2019 2020 2021 2022 / 10 9 8 7 6 5 4 3 2 1

ISBN: 978-0-8478-6550-5
Library of Congress Control Number: 2019937696

Visit us online:
Facebook.com/RizzoliNewYork
Twitter: @Rizzoli_Books
Instagram.com/RizzoliBooks
Pinterest.com/RizzoliBooks
Youtube.com/user/RizzoliNY
Issuu.com/Rizzoli

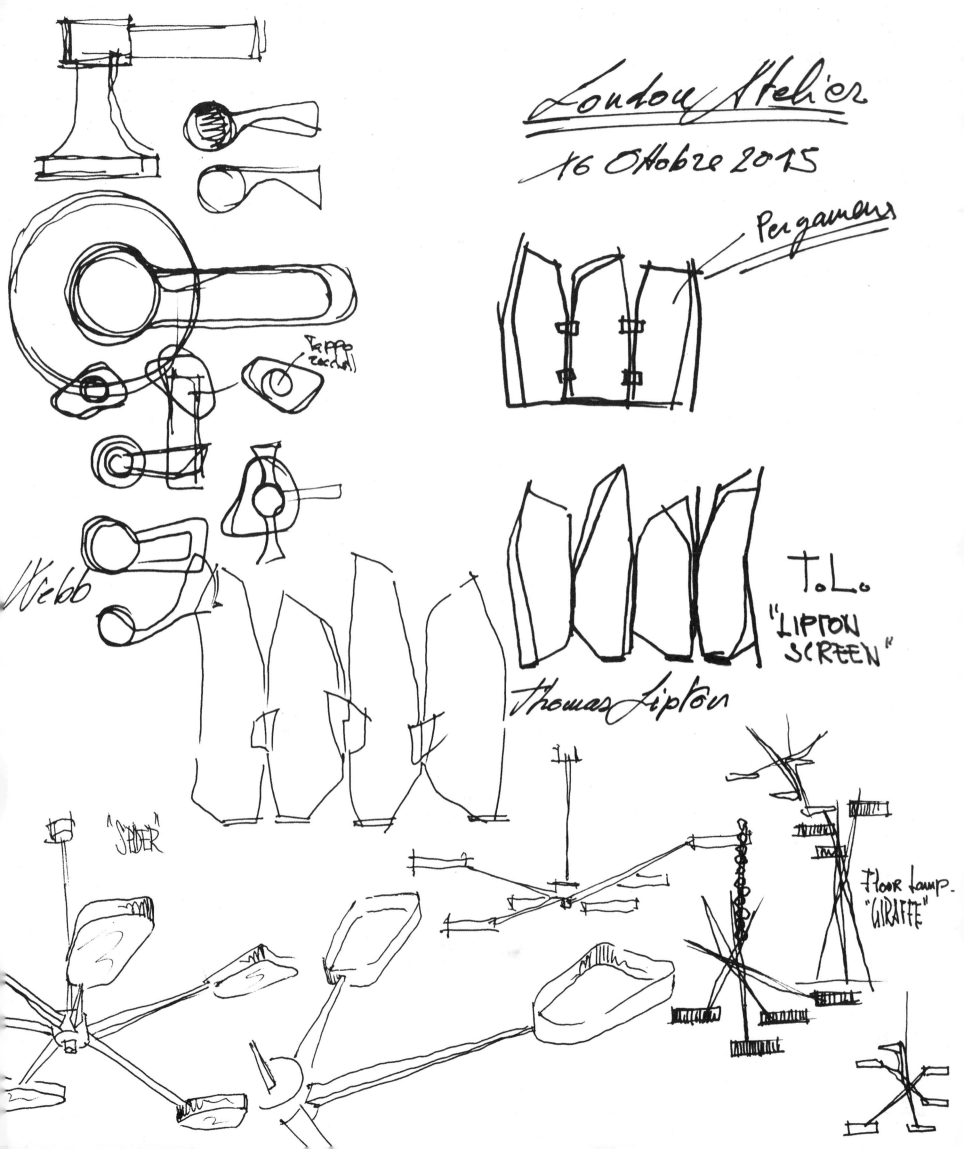

London Atelier
16 Ottobre 2015

Pergamena

Peppo zocchi

Webb

Thomas Lipton

T.L.
"LIPTON SCREEN"

"SPIDER"

Floor lamp.
"GIRAFFE"